I'm Sober...So Now What?

A Journey of Hope and Healing

D1319294

I'm Sober...So Now What?

A Journey of Hope and Healing

Melissa Gissy Witherspoon

Marylee,

So grateful for our Connection!
you bring so much love &
beauty to our world.
Keep Shining your light.

Peace be with you

2022 Non-Fiction: Inspiration

2023 Non-Fiction: Health & Wellness - Addiction & Recovery

2023 Non-Fiction: Self-Help - Inspiration

I'm Sober...So Now What?

A Journey of Hope and Healing

Copyright © 2023 Melissa Gissy Witherspoon
ISBN:979-8-9876925-0-9

Foreword by Gary Chapman, author of *The 5 Love Languages*
Edited by Elizabeth Maynard-Garrett, Polish Point Editing
Cover Art by Bryan Williams

Published by
Sober-Now
Winston-Salem, North Carolina
United States of America
www.sober-now.com

With gratitude, proceeds from
the sale of this book will be given back
to the sober community.

Pay it forward:

If you would like to share my message of hope
with others, scan the QR code below
to make a donation to Sober-Now.

Funds raised will provide copies of this
book to recovery centers, the incarcerated,
sober living, safe houses, and those
who cannot afford a copy.

Dedication

*This book is dedicated to every person whose
life has been impacted by addiction.*

*Also, to my four children, Tyler, Hailey, Caroline, and Jake,
my love for you is endless. You have inspired me to
become a better person and live a sober life.*

*And to my family and friends who loved me and
believed in me when I did not.*

*Last, but not least, to my husband, Derek, who brought me
to the steps of recovery and held my hand through them
even during the times it would have been easier to give up.*

Acknowledgements

Special thanks to each of the following individuals who
played key roles in bringing this book to completion:

Father Peter Nouck
Victoria Meyers
Rachel Keener
Dr. William Casey
Bryan Williams
Elizabeth M. Garrett
Dr. Gary Chapman

Without your encouragement and prayers,
this book wouldn't have come to fruition:

Sarah Bradford Croom
Mary Lynn England
Tina Arcaro McDonald
Suzanne Caroon
Joanna Eccles
Teddy Grabowski
Chip & MaryFaith Stone
Jennifer Barlow
Father Brian Cook
Father Michael Buttner
Hank & Tina Rudge

About the Cover Art

The Path by Bryan Williams

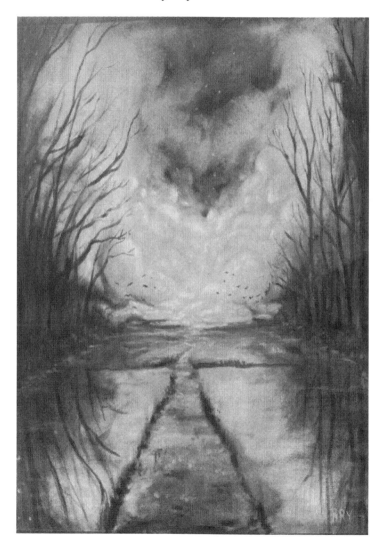

A letter of interpretation from the artist:

I felt, after reading your book, that your path or others' paths can be represented in this painting. The trees on each side represent the things in life trying to tempt or trick you off your path of healing.

The path in the center leads you to the light but you always have those temptations on each side, leaning in toward you.

If you just keep staying your course, sooner or later you will reach the light or happiness or heavens. The light continues to be your focus ahead of you. Darkness cannot live in the presence of light, so the path leads you to the light.

I felt like the reflections in the ice on each side of you are important because in order to find acceptance and make changes in your life, you obviously have to reflect, and you also have to be precise in your decision-making and intentions for each day to stay on that path. The sides of the path are thin ice. This represents how careful you must be as you walk on your journey.

Toward the end of the path, I broke the trees off into birds to symbolize your new freedom. The birds represent the breakthrough or change in your life, and they fly ahead of you, drawing you to them continuously.

The painting is your point of view while standing on the path. It's hard for me to see you ahead of yourself. This is why I left your actual body out of the picture. The painting shows that you're coming up to a crossroads, symbolizing that you have choices as well and you are changing along your journey.

www.facebook.com/BrytheArtist

Table of Contents

Foreword

Millions of families have experienced the impact of alcohol and drug addiction. Sometimes it is young children whose childhood is stolen by addicted parents. Sometimes it is teenagers whose future is side-tracked by addiction. Then there are young adults whose addiction has caused great pain to their parents. Many jobs have been lost and career dreams put on hold while the one who is addicted seeks help.

As a marriage and family counselor for more than forty years, few things have brought more tears to my eyes than the stories of fractured relationships due to drug and alcohol addiction. Perhaps the only thing that is even more painful is the number of deaths that are the results of such addictions. Sometimes it is the death of children and adults who are killed in an automobile accident caused by someone driving under the influence. Thousands of addicts also die a premature death because of drug and alcohol abuse.

In the midst of the darkness, the good news is, there is help. Alcoholics Anonymous, and treatment centers are available throughout the country. For family members of the addict, there are organizations like Al-Anon available to help them understand how best to walk with the addict. Thousands of individuals have found help and sobriety by taking first steps with such organizations. I have always had deep admiration for those who invest their lives in these organizations. The road to sobriety is a journey and the addict needs fellow travelers who can give guidance and encouragement.

The book you hold in your hand is written by one who has walked and is walking this journey. It is her deep desire to help others who are walking the road to sobriety and life beyond. She shares her own rock bottom experience with addiction and her journey to a meaningful life serving God by serving others. She does not suggest a magic formula for instant success but is realistic in sharing her own journey and identifying practical steps along the road to a life worth living.

If you are addicted, the first step is to admit the truth about the power of alcohol and drugs on your life. If you are struggling with admitting the truth, or if you already recognize your need for help, this book is for you. If you are already involved with Alcoholics Anonymous or some other helpful organization, you will find this book a welcome companion.

While this book is written to the addict, it speaks also to the loved ones of the addict. The author purposefully includes information that will give direction and hope to the family and friends of someone in addiction. We all want to help those who are struggling with addiction, but sometimes we need insight in how best to help. I believe this book will give you that insight.

Gary Chapman, Ph.D.
Author of *The 5 Love Languages*

Introduction

"You should write a book," they say. "You have a message," they say. I can't even write a text message without arguing with my phone that the word "their" is really spelled that way or should I be using "they're" or "there" instead? Wait, what was I texting in the first place? I'm guilty of typing and clicking send without proofing it and slowing down to make sure auto correct hasn't changed one of my random thoughts into a dirty sentence before I hit the send button. Yes, that's right. I have clicked send on a message to my mother-in-law asking her if she was still feeling sick and it changed it to are you sure you like... well, you get the point.

Even after several years of sobriety, being in the moment, slowing it down, "easy does it," has continued to be one of my biggest challenges. I rush from work to barely make it to carpool so I can get groceries in time to half-make what I interpret as a reasonable weeknight dinner that never gets eaten because the rest of my family is tired of the four meals I have been cycling through over the past few years.

I haven't ever in my forty-plus years enjoyed reading. I read to my children because that is what "good moms" are supposed to do and the kids seem to enjoy it. Nothing gives me more pleasure these days than pleasing my children. I have spent most of my life winging it off of *Cliff Notes* or book summaries and watching the movie instead of reading the book.

And thank God for Google and spell check. But let me be clear, I am not grateful for text message auto correct. That one is a thorn in my texting finger! The mere fact that someone would assume I would be capable of writing something longer than a to-do list on a sticky note pad makes me want to crawl outside of my own skin.

My writing this book began with a priest named Father Peter Nouck. A jolly man from Cameroon, his infectious laugh can leave you with a grin that almost hurts your face even on your worst day. He makes it a habit to check in with me frequently to see how I'm coming along on my sobriety journey. He insists on me writing a book to fellow alcoholics and believes there is someone who will read my book who will need to hear my message.

My initial response to him was, "I'm a high school dropout who only recently obtained her GED because it was court-ordered during my DUI Court program. I have no titles to claim for my reason to write and no formal education to help the reader trust that I'm worthy of their precious time reading my words." His response was, "That's a good story Melissa. You will put that in your book."

Next came, Rachel, first an acquaintance, now a dear friend. She is the mother of my youngest son's best friend. Since my life currently revolves around work and my children, my closest friends have become either co-workers or moms of my children's friends. I learned after a few years of running into Rachel at birthday parties or play dates that she is a published author—the kind I'm not, like I mentioned to Father Peter—college educated from a prestigious school, an avid reader who is Christ-centered and always knew she would write. At first, our conversations focused on how things were going, you know... surface level, funny things kids do and say. Then, one day on her driveway for no particular reason, I can remember blurting out my recovery story, the abbreviated version, and she said, "You should write a book."

As wind caused tree branches to sweep the ground, I stood there with a blank stare on my face and crickets chirping in my brain. My mouth uttered the redundant conversation I had been having with Father Peter for months. She shared that she wrote books and her reasons for writing. But as she spoke, all I could think of after I left her driveway was where I could pull the car over so I could Google her name and find out more about this intriguing woman who thinks my story should be told.

Once I finally did, awe and maybe some embarrassment engulfed me when I saw what an established and amazing writer my humble friend was. And since that windy day on her driveway, our friendship has grown from that one authentic conversation. Yes, now another person holds me accountable for sharing my message.

"Get familiar with books," she said. So, I did, reluctantly. Eventually, I gobbled up any book mentioned or passed in front of me. Some I would start and never finish, and some I couldn't put down. I even went as far as downloading audio books because much of my time is spent shuttling kids to and from places or tracking back and forth from my home in North Carolina to Georgia where I visit my two older children and family. But I have never talked myself in and out of something as much as I have with this book idea.

After several months of self-deprecating talks in my head, I thought I had the cure for how I could finally put this outrageous idea to rest. I planned to approach my husband with this ludicrous idea, and he would shoot it down straight away. He would tell me in his logical and practical manner that there was no time for such nonsense and that I was under-qualified for such a task.

But he didn't do that at all. His eyes glowing with pride and his voice filled with compassion, he said, "I think you can do it. There is someone who will benefit from it. After all, isn't that what all this hard work in recovery is about?"

He followed it up with some ridiculous joke because that is how we have learned to handle deep talks in our relationship over the years. I don't remember the joke, only the slow, steady tone in his voice and the look in his eyes when he spoke to me. The man who saved my life by leading me to the beginning steps of my sobriety journey and who struggled with resentment since I returned home sober, had given me encouragement to pursue it! Even then, I resisted every sign and gift God had sent me.

It wasn't until I met a Dr. Bill Casey that I fully accepted the challenge. I "accidentally" (I'm beginning to understand by this point that there are no accidents when God has orchestrated a plan.) ran into him in a tiny library at church as he placed his very own book on the shelf. I began asking questions, and again, projectile vomited my entire story about sobriety, along with this crazy book idea... to a complete stranger!

It felt like I was an outsider watching myself share my story. My mind tried to stop me, although every fiber of my being jolted me forward. I even cried... like the ugly cry where you sob and snot pours like a faucet out of your nose, and you can't catch your breath. I was completely vulnerable in front of this man I knew nothing about.

Somehow, I knew the Holy Spirit was sucking my fears and insecurities out of my physical body and delivering them to this man for me. I asked for help and had no clue he himself had been on a writing journey and lived to tell about it. The conversation shared that day and the look in his eyes told me God was using him to speak to me about a purpose.

So, if that brief, "chance" meeting in a tiny library at church had such an impact on me, why couldn't a few pages written by an uneducated, recovering alcoholic impact another person? Could it be that someone might need to hear that life after drinking or any traumatic event is possible and can be quite beautiful?

In my meager attempt at obedience, I sat and wrote in the car while my daughter was at softball practice. I could only assume having to drive to a practice field an hour from home to a location with no phone service or internet connection was another gift from God so I could have time on a weekly basis to focus on writing.

And why after several prompts did I finally put pen to paper? You deserve to know that you are not alone and that your journey, although painstaking, ugly, and seemingly impossible at times, is not impossible at all. You can find a way to maneuver through this life on life's terms without masking all the feelings and emotions with alcohol. You can celebrate the accomplishments along the way and take the reprieve God grants us in between each heartache that life delivers so we are ready to endure the next proverbial hill we must climb.

I do not claim to have the answers. My wings are just beginning to unfold out of the cocoon into this new life that has clearly been designed for me by a divine love. On a good day I don't even know where I set my coffee cup or remember my kids' names as I'm yelling down the stairs for them to get their shoes on because we are running late (again)!

But I am certain of one thing—out of the estimated 88,000 people who die from alcohol- related causes annually, making alcohol the third leading preventable cause of death in the United States, you deserve to know you have a purpose, you are not alone, and you are loved.

How can I love you and not know you? Ah... but in some sense, I do know you. Perhaps our circumstances are not the exact same, but the paths we chose to be an alcoholic, followed by pursuing recovery and living a fulfilled life while managing our disease will forever be a bond that cannot be understood by just anyone. Without ever meeting each other, God has granted us a fraternity or a sisterhood if you will, that reminds us we never have to feel alone again.

With that, I welcome you to join me in the next few pages to discover some of my challenges through recovery, the beauty that unfolded through those challenges, and the pain one feels without the substance to mask it. If you get nothing but a good laugh or cry while reading this, I am grateful for your time.

I hope you can pick it up and put it down, then pick it back up again whenever you need it. I hope the exact page you needed to read speaks to your soul and gets you from the "one day at a time" to the next. If nothing else, I have embraced promise five of the Alcoholics Anonymous Twelve-step Promises: "No matter how far down the scale we have gone, we will see that our experience can benefit others."

Chapter One

My Name is Melissa, and I'm an Alcoholic

I suppose before I dive into sharing with you what sobriety looks like for me, I should give you a glimpse of my journey to rock bottom. If you are reading this and are not in recovery or you are contemplating recovery but haven't had the chance to attend an Alcoholics Anonymous (AA) meeting, I should share with you that the chips I mention in this chapter refer to the poker chips you receive for milestones reached in your recovery.

The first chip, the one where you stand in front of a room filled with fellow alcoholics and admit you are ready to stop drinking, is white. It takes courage and strength just to walk into a meeting room of strangers and be vulnerable. But to stand up in front of that group of alcoholics, strangers meeting together from all different walks of life looking for one common purpose, to stop drinking, is one of the hardest and bravest steps you will take in your sobriety. I am no one-chip wonder. This means I didn't receive a white chip, get sober, and live happily ever after. Like just about everything else in my life, it took me several attempts before I was ready to make a commitment and do the work.

My dance in and out of the AA rooms started with attending meetings with a boyfriend over two decades ago. He was ready to admit he was powerless over alcohol and that his life had become unmanageable. I was smitten with him but I had no intentions of joining his journey. I was just there to be with him and support him. I wasn't powerless over alcohol, not in my mind anyway. "I have Italian and Irish genes. We just like to drink," I would always say.

I came from a family that had several functional alcoholics. Alcohol was served at just about any event I attended, including church, and most of my friends and coworkers throughout my life drank heavily. Most social events would start with "pre-gaming" as we would call it and carried all the way through the event until I puked or passed out. Then the next day we would all put the pieces together of the night before and have a good laugh at our shenanigans, usually while partaking in "the hair of the dog that bit us." If a dinner had ended and someone left the table with alcohol remaining in their glass, I would down it and say something clever like, "Waste not, want not, let me help you get your money's worth, or it's five o'clock somewhere."

That level of drinking defined my normal. In my mind I wasn't in trouble like the boyfriend. I had a job, owned a home while most people my age still lived with their parents, and took nice vacations. I had a bank account that stayed at a comfortable balance, and my family had not turned on me like his had. Occasionally I wandered across the hall to the Al-Anon meeting room because one could only assume if *he* was the alcoholic then *I* was in need of support for loving the alcoholic. Al-Anon is a support group to help families of alcoholics. In my mind I controlled every aspect of my life.

I knew when I made a bad choice, and I always had backup plans and answers for any situation I could get myself into... or so I thought. I spent the early part of my life learning how to weave in and out of things. I became so good at it that I was most often commended for my efforts. "You'd make a great attorney," or "You'll be a real estate mogul one day." My favorite one was, "Melissa, you could sell ice to an Eskimo."

I was never deemed the smart one. Instead, I struggled in school due to an undiagnosed learning disorder. Alternative learning programs for my generation rarely existed. You either stayed with the class or got left behind. I actually had a teacher tell me on more than one occasion that I would never amount to anything in society. After you hear that so many times you begin to believe it.

When offered an IQ assessment as part of a recovery program, I found out that I actually have a reasonably high IQ level, which isn't too surprising, I suppose, since I come from a family of several intellectuals. Most are very successful in their own endeavors. I always felt inferior around most of them. I'm not sure if it was my timing in family conversations or my lack of knowledge about the subjects they would talk about, but anytime I would try and engage, it would earn me strange looks. I always assumed it was because I lacked intellect.

To this day, I feel awkward in most social settings. I get anxious, overthinking and blurting out things that normal people know not to say. I'm quite shy and insecure, so in order to survive, I developed skills to present myself as outgoing, sometimes... okay most times, overdoing it to compensate for the insecurities that fester inside of me.

That inner voice you have—I have one, too—but it gets quieted by the rackets and scenarios I create in my mind. That's where "liquid courage" (vodka) came into play—to help me take the edge off, calming my thoughts so I could focus on the perfect thing to say to someone. I became a walking, talking salesman, perfecting charm and wit down to a science.

The words "Perfect Art of Deflection" should have been tattooed on my forehead, but that would have impeded my aesthetics I worked on so diligently in order to tie my charming little package all together. Instead, I got a boob job, Botox and lip fillers, and an eating disorder.

I also picked up a couple of tattoos along my journey although neither has any significance. They were just desperate attempts to get some guy's attention or to claim some sense of individualism. The clownfish on my hip has since morphed into a blowfish after several pregnancies, and the Indian feathers on my ankle have faded and now look like a blurry, elongated tarantula. I guess I achieved my goal of individualism because I am almost certain I am the only one who can claim these ridiculous unidentifiable ink blobs as my own.

One fateful night though, in my early twenties, just barely old enough to drink legally, I received my first citation for "Driving under the Influence," better known as a DUI. My manipulation skills that had always gotten me everything I thought I ever wanted and out of everything I thought I didn't want, had no chance against Cobb County's Finest.

I had ended a night of binge drinking at a slew of bars in a prominent party area called Buckhead. While racing home to beat the sunrise, I drove ninety-five miles per hour down Interstate 75 with the top down on my silver convertible in the middle of winter. I felt carefree and knew no pain, thanks to dirty martinis and shots of whatever from whomever was buying that night.

This poor decision making earned me a DUI conviction and a court order to attend AA meetings, along with several other activities like spending time in jail and attending a defensive driving course. I returned to the AA rooms, and this time I picked up that white chip.

I believe my alcoholism really began years prior to that incident. My life took a turn in my late teens with one decision, and I never got back on track. I dropped out of high school and found myself running with a crowd who introduced me to a world that felt similar to Never-Never Land in *Peter Pan*—a bunch of adults acting like kids living life to the fullest with no regard for anyone but themselves. Life reflected an ongoing den of iniquity, a party from sun up to sun down, complete with VIP sections at clubs and restaurants, along with fancy, fast cars. I went along for the ride from the get-go.

Almost immediately, I met the main drug dealers, the top dogs. I didn't look or act like the groupies who lingered around them. At the time I wasn't an addict so I wasn't a threat... just fresh, new to the scene, and young, able to bounce around the room using my charm to entertain and keep the environment fun and engaging. I was offered a free place to stay and found this entire experience exhilarating, like a scene straight out of a modern-day gangster movie.

In reality, though, this is where you can insert that I was a run-away and under-age drinker with a fake ID, using cocaine, frequenting strip clubs, and eventually being held against my will for days. Some call this human trafficking, but I call it rape. I suppose human trafficking is the more commonly used term nowadays, but I can assure you it has been around for a long time and is what taught me very early on that sex could be used for power.

Regardless of what you want to label it, it wasn't at all what I had signed up for. But like a moth caught in a spider's web, I could not break free. The more the moth fights the web, the more it gets tangled until the moth tires out and has no choice but to lay there and await its doom.

I was beaten so badly that I was sent to the hospital. I was smart enough to tell the doctor the truth.... you know... that I fell down a flight of stairs and wasn't able to break my fall with my hands, so I caught myself with my face. This became a theme in most of my relationships that followed.

Eventually the police caught on. Detectives contacted my parents to let them know they had wire taps at the place where I stayed. They were concerned I was in danger, but would not disclose the location because they planned a raid. I suppose it was more important to them to have more time to build a case than it was to rescue me or allow my parents to rescue me.

When the police moved in, nobody did like in the movies where they scatter like cockroaches. Instead, some went to jail, and others were rescued. I was one of the rescued, but would never be the same. Several of those people have since died, a couple are living clean lives, and some are in jail. I escaped that life and went back to my parents' home, with most of my family and friends never being the wiser about my experience over those few, life-changing months.

My innocence was lost. I had made choices during that time which mirrored signing my soul over to the devil. To this day, I rarely speak on the events that took place in the condo on Powers Ferry Road. It's still hard to talk or even think about them. Fear grips my soul as I write this section for you to read, but I know in my heart that, in order for you to understand my past, I have to share it with you.

I also know it will be an important piece of my own healing, or at least that's what I have been told. Right now, in this particular moment, I feel reluctant, raw, and vulnerable which is usually how I feel at the beginning of any healing process. Those feelings must be felt without substances though, so let's press on, together, shall we?

I had planned to move forward with my life as if none of this ever happened. All the while, the deal I made with the devil hid in my tortured soul, popping up at unsolicited times reminding me that shame and fear owned me now. I pushed through the next two decades of my life with force just trying to get to the place that would make me feel happy and whole. I drank more and more through the process, weaving in and out of abusive relationships. I fell into a rabbit hole of choices and circumstances that led to more choices and circumstances. You get the point, I'm sure.

I managed to rack up six engagement rings and blow through two marriages, as well as countless jobs in the restaurant industry and property management, leaving three children most of the time without a consistent mother. When I was around them, I either drank or had a hangover. I offered them no quality time filled with happy memories. Instead, life was a constant struggle with superficial successes. I masked all of the emotional pain with drugs and alcohol because I felt mostly guilt and shame for not being what I always thought a good mother should be.

The actual details of the two decades that led to my rock bottom perhaps would make this book more interesting. However, my point is not to romanticize my journey to rock bottom or to harm anyone I have already made amends with, but rather share that I didn't just wake up one day and say, "I think I'll be an alcoholic today."

Sure, it was my choice. My own free will led me here. Many factors over the years and my lack of reasonable cognitive thinking from a very early age helped contribute to my poor decisions, making my path crooked at best.

Chapter Two

A Divine Intervention

I fell in and out of the AA rooms for twenty years, but it wasn't until after my fourth child was born that I once again picked up a white chip and started working the steps. And even then, I spent almost a year in and out of rehab and jail before a divine intervention took place.

This was my toughest pregnancy physically and emotionally. I was on bed rest for most of it, so depression kicked in well before he was born. Bed rest is meant for the mother to stay still and rest while her child grows inside her womb. To me, bed rest felt like being robbed of everything I had built around me to make my life appear perfect.

Overnight my career in property management, my freedom to attend family functions, and my ability to do my part as a mother and wife were stripped away. I was being forced to sit with myself day in and day out while the rest of the world went on around me and without me.

Sure, my family and friends were extremely supportive, doing their best to fill the gaps where I could no longer be present. But the part that caused me so much anxiety and depression was the immediate loss of control that I thought I had finally started to feel in life. And even worse, I had to be with myself, by myself for great lengths of time. That meant hours and days of thinking and feeling emotions with no ability or idea of how to process any of it. My fallback crutch of "drinking on it" to get through the pain wasn't available to me, so the depression took hold of me stronger and harder than ever.

After my son was born, my OB/GYN thought Xanax would be a great cure for my post-partum depression. It only took a hot second for me to decide that eating Xanax like they were Tic Tac breath mints and chasing them with vodka would be a wise decision. After a few months of enjoying my new lethal cocktail, I got another DUI and a short stint in outpatient therapy, which eventually led me to a thirty-day treatment facility I actually attended for fifty-five days.

Clearly, I wasn't ready to leave rehab because I relapsed within twenty-four hours. I arrived home on a Sunday night, and by Monday morning I stopped by a liquor store on my way from an AA meeting. At that moment in the liquor store parking lot, while downing my airplane bottles of apple vodka (because, you know, apple flavor makes it less easy to detect the smell -not true), I realized I was very sick, and inevitably, I would die from my disease. At some point over the next few days, I decided to speed up the slow, agonizing death process and started planning a good solid go at ending it all.

With a final note written, house clean, and everything in order so I could leave this world behind, I gobbled handfuls of pills I obtained from my recent trip to rehab. I'm still not sure why I thought a clean house would ease the pain of my loved ones finding my lifeless body, but that represents my manic drug-infused state at the time.

On a side note, I'm still perplexed why neither I nor my husband questioned why, after treatment for alcohol, they sent me home with a large plastic bag filled with sleeping pills, muscle relaxers, and other narcotics an addict has no business being prescribed. Nevertheless, I washed them down with a good liter of vodka and cut my wrists. But my attempt failed. Yes, I even failed at suicide.

People have said to me, "Maybe you didn't really want to die" or "Maybe you were just seeking attention." That wasn't the case at all. I was ready to go. I really was. Exhausted and filled with pain, I had grown weary of looking into the eyes of people I loved, seeing their pain, and knowing I caused it.

So, I lay on the cold, hard floor of my unfinished basement, with a toxic amount of alcohol and prescription drugs in my body. I had always been terrified to go into that basement for fear of a rodent or camelback cricket crossing my path. But that afternoon, only one thing filled my mind... escaping from the pain forever.

Oddly enough, I placed an old comforter beneath me so the mess would be easier to clean up. I took long, deep breaths knowing they would be my last. I remember thinking the stale, musty stench of that dark, cold basement symbolized the stench that was to come when I would soon enter the gates of hell. I burned a candle next to me so I could light my menthol cigarettes. I assumed it would be difficult to operate a cigarette lighter properly while trying to die so I wanted to be prepared. I had the Beatles' song "Let It Be" playing on repeat. It is still one of my favorite songs but I hear the words so differently these days. I faded in and out but I wasn't dying, not fast enough anyway.

I screamed (most likely slurring loudly) to the mother of all mothers, "Mother Mary! Why keep me here to be in pain and cause so much pain to others? Just take me and send me straight to hell where I belong!" I repeated it over and over. And then... I saw something.

Now mind you, I was not only in a state of desperation, but highly intoxicated. Hallucinating could possibly be the explanation if you aren't ready to buy into what I'm about to share with you. Maybe it was all of the smoke collecting in one spot from the cigarettes I lit back-to-back. You and I could come up with all sorts of explanations I am sure, but I know in my heart that I saw something, and I heard a voice. It told me that if I would completely turn my will over to God, that I would be free and that I was supposed to be alive... that I had a purpose to fulfill and it would all eventually make sense if I could trust in my creator even when it felt impossible to do so.

It's hard to explain how I heard it. It wasn't like what it would be if you and I were having a conversation with each other. It was a voice I could hear deep inside of me. The figure talked to me but the mouth didn't move. I felt a warm hug, and love shot through my veins.

Imagine being warmed from the inside out, feeling no pain, just a calm, steady flow of energy and love. The most intense feeling of love I had ever felt engulfed me, and I have not felt that same feeling since. Soon after, my husband returned home unexpectedly to get something he had forgotten. I suppose the overwhelming stench of cigarette smoke wafting from the frightful basement ratted me out... He found my seemingly lifeless body.

It's strange to me that for so many years I had lost faith in God, and at what I thought was the hour of my death, I turned to Him, specifically to the mother of His only son, Jesus. For so long vodka and Xanax had become my god, my higher power. When you live so many years in guilt and shame how could God possibly love me?

That question lay at the core of the rabbit hole I fell down—a dialectical dance of two questions. How could God ever have allowed such painful things to happen to me? And how could He ever love me for the choices I made through my painful experiences? Throw a dash of self-will run-riot into the mix, and you, my friend, have my personal recipe for rock bottom. Where I am now in my life, I understand that He was with me all along. But jails, institutions, and near-death lay at the bottom of my rabbit hole where I would have to walk through them in order to begin my spiritual awakening.

I had exhausted every friendship. My family had given up all hope, and my older two children no longer wished to see me. After leaving rehab just two weeks prior, relapsing, accumulating three more DUIs in that time frame, and failing miserably at trying to take my own life, back to rehab I went. And there, I picked up yet another white chip. It was the last to be picked up. I say that, knowing with my disease, I am always one drink away from returning to a life of past days... one sip and I'm back to another white chip, if I'm lucky.

Chapter Three

One Day at a Time

During treatment "One day at a time" is the phrase that was pounded into every fiber of my being. I couldn't ask what's for breakfast the next day or what movie will be playing in the gathering room of my treatment facility without someone saying, "Just for today Melissa," "One day at a time, Melissa," "Easy does it, Melissa." That's what everyone told me over, and over, and over.

I get it now, although it remains a daily challenge. Back then I thought *what in the world is wrong with people that I can't ask about a menu choice for tomorrow or movie choice a few days away?! What's the big frigging deal?!* I would eventually learn that the big frigging deal was that essentially anything you reach for in the future while trying not to drink in the present is an unnecessary distraction. It simply doesn't matter because it hasn't happened yet. Also, you do not have the ability to balance both present and future at the same time, especially while harbouring resentments from the past.

For a woman who had no idea how to be present in the moment, "one day at a time" sounded like a foreign language every time someone said it. I was actually quite annoyed with the catch phrase at that point. I mean, you tell me how to focus on one day at a time when I'm still sitting in my past mistakes and resentments while looking forward at calendars filled with outpatient treatment appointments, drug tests, court dates, jail time, and family and criminal attorney meetings. But that's exactly how it happened, one-day-at-a-time.

I'm not going to sugar coat it either. I experienced one long, relentless, painstaking, hard day at a time. Some days I would "clock watch" just as I would when drinking. You know, I would do laundry and clean breakfast dishes and vacuum, then I deserved to take a drink or I'd drop off kids at school and head to work to do a report, then I'd get to pop a Xanax and down it with a gulp of wine disguised in my coffee mug. It was a game of watching the clock to get through each day with a reward system.

Old habits don't break easy. In the beginning, I essentially did the same thing. But my sober clock watching looked like getting something accomplished, then checking the clock to see the countdown of how much closer I was to going to sleep and finishing another day without taking a drink. That was the only game plan that would get me through what was to come in my first year of sobriety.

I was only days into yet another attempt at recovery when I discovered the thing that would eventually propel me through my first year. All the other things I walked through are just as important to my story, but this one launched the spiritual awakening I was promised on my cold, hard basement floor that day I tried to take my life.

I sat in an isolation unit in rehab recovering from an emergency tonsillectomy and the flu. The only thing worse than having your tonsils removed as an adult and having the flu at the same time is recovering from a tonsillectomy and the flu at a rehab facility during Christmas with no family or friends and not being able to take pain medication because you are trying to get sober. But I recovered. I made it through every painful swallow of Jell-O and Gatorade and was moved from the infirmary back to the general population to continue my treatment just in time to learn that my dad had stage four pancreatic cancer and was given a few weeks to live. He was going to die before I could know him sober, really sober.

I remember exactly where I stood when I received the phone call from my dad. As soon as the call ended, I fell to my knees, tears streaming my face, and cried out, "Okay God, I'm doing what you ask of me and now this is my reward?"

He didn't answer me. If He did, I wasn't in a place emotionally or spiritually where I would have heard it. I was still talking at Him, not to Him. And in that moment, I was mad at Him.

A couple of days later, I graduated from the program. I remember standing there at the graduation ceremony with no family or friends, thinking, "Well, if and when Dad dies, he won't miss moments like this. He will be able to look down at what I am up to, I guess." It sounds like a weird, morbid thought to have while everyone else in the room smiled with pride for their accomplishments and celebrated with loved ones. Looking back, I think I was trying to wrap my head around the loss that was coming and trying to find a comfortable spot or some form of acceptance with it.

I remember how excited everyone was to graduate and get home to start their new sober lives. Not me. I was terrified. My new lease on life looked daunting and impossible to tackle. I had to leave my safe space where I made so much progress to return to all the mess I had left behind.

That's right, my friend, there would be no proverbial pink cloud for me. I wasn't going to get to walk out of rehab and back into life with that renewed sense of purpose like most people talk about.

They say the recovery pink cloud makes the air smell different, grass looks greener, everything is almost overwhelmingly happy and wonderful because you see things through eyes that are no longer foggy by substance abuse.

Those experiences I heard about in meetings and groups were going to be for others in recovery. I had wreaked too much havoc prior to my final attempt at sobriety to enjoy that fresh start.

When I returned home, I was going to bury my dad and face the wreckage from my past. My new lease on life was going to resemble purgatory—a purgatory that sat closer to Hell than it did Heaven. I was going to feel more pain than I had ever known, and this time I was going to feel every bit of it because I wasn't protected by my precious prize in a glass bottle marked vodka.

Life on life's terms hit me before I left the treatment center, and over the next year, I found myself repeating the questions, "This is supposed to be a better way of life? This is what I get for doing the next right thing?"

I had played victim for decades, so my mentality during the first year of sobriety was still very much in that same spot. I had done the work to get my body clean and began the process of dissecting my disease and how I had gotten to that point. But I had not had enough time under my belt to do the work that peels back all the dead layers covering my soul.

You may have heard the term "dry drunk," which is a term that describes an alcoholic who no longer drinks but maintains the same behavior patterns of an alcoholic. I was in a healing limbo so to speak, and in due time, the processes would require me to start exercising my ability to live life in a "woke state." Until that time, I would have to focus on two things, waking up sober and going to bed sober.

My daily routine of wake-up calls, breakfast hall, meditation, yoga, group therapy, one-on-one therapy, journaling, and forty-something smoke breaks in between was interrupted with news of devastating events occurring in the outside world while I was in my rehab bubble just trying not to feel like I wanted to die.

As if my dad dying and me facing two years in prison for criminal charges in my habitual violator case for multiple DUI's strewn across north Georgia wasn't enough, my third child, my daughter, had been abruptly removed from our home while I was in treatment to live at her grandmother's house.

My two older children lived with my first ex-husband and his family. My third child had been with me by my side her entire life. Her biological father was in jail for a probation violation, and I was in treatment for drugs and alcohol. This left a window of opportunity for her paternal grandmother to finally gain control and rip my daughter out of her home.

Now she lived away from the only real dad she had ever known... the one who had always been her safe place and gotten her to and from school, sports, and play dates when her biological father could only visit under supervised visitation, and her mom was too busy playing victim and drinking on it.

The ex-mother-in-law who assured me on phone calls from treatment that she would work with my husband, supporting him with care for my daughter while her son was in jail and I was in treatment, planned the entire time to gain emergency custody.

I've never heard her reasoning. Maybe she was mad that her own child was in trouble and "taken away from her?" Maybe she was afraid of how I would be when I got out of treatment... would I repeat mistakes that caused her granddaughter emotional harm and create an unsafe environment? Maybe she heard we might move to North Carolina where my husband's family lived to have a fresh start, and she didn't want to lose her granddaughter in that process. Maybe it was a little of all things mentioned, but the cold, hard fact was she did it in such an abrupt and deceitful way that it left me shocked and confused, my husband heartbroken and helpless.

My husband had done nothing wrong. He was not an alcoholic. He rarely even drank. He was the one who held a steady job, cared for our infant son, and raised my daughter as if she was his own flesh and blood, continuously pushing for my recovery when all others had given up. He didn't sign up for any of the things he walked through although he was doing it, balancing it all, and doing a fine job.

The loophole was that my husband and I were only common law married at this point. He had gone through a program called RCIA to become Catholic, with my dad as his sponsor, so we could have a wedding—one blessed by God in a church, a holy sacrament. Not a marriage at a courthouse like I had done in the past. I never knew what true love was and always believed he would probably leave me one day. He would figure out I was a fraud, pack his bags, and hit the road faster than the Road Runner zipping away from Wylie Coyote.

That's funny, isn't it? This man was willing to change religion, cashed in his 401k to help pay for multiple treatment facilities, raised a child from another man, never considering her as anything but his own, and tried his best to figure out his role as a stepdad with the older two kids who had a present father and extended family in their lives. All that, and I never could accept that he loved me.

We had started planning a church wedding for after our son was born, but my rock bottom got in the way, and the wedding never came to fruition. So, he was presented by the ex-mother-in-law to the judge as a live-in boyfriend, and she was able to obtain an emergency temporary order of custody.

The court didn't know at the time it wasn't in my daughter's best interest to be taken from the only man who was a real parental figure to her for most of her life and to remove her from her siblings, her home, her friends, and her softball team (Softball still remains her constant, but you can read about that when she writes her own book one day). Those details weren't provided to the judge. The court only knew the mom was a drunk back in rehab after several failed attempts, who faced several years in prison for her drinking and driving offenses, and that the biological father was back in jail on a violation of probation, facing several years behind bars as well.

We would have to get me home from treatment and go to court and prove our case in order to get her back. And just before that court date, we would rush to the courthouse and get married so the man who was very much a part of what was going on, would be considered during the entire custody process.

Those first two weeks home from treatment without her were agonizing. I literally felt like a piece of my being had been ripped out of me. Every day I wished I could have a drink to endure the pain, but I knew I had to stay sober long enough to get her home.

● ● ●

My husband worked from home to help get attorneys lined up for all my upcoming court cases and continued caring for our children while I re-acclimated myself to real life and the series of events that came with it.

It just so happened that the family law attorney he hired while I was still in treatment was best friends with a criminal attorney. They both worked diligently together to get things moving on all of my pending cases. Since my driver's license had been revoked, he would work with my dad, mom, sister, and his mom to create a schedule to get me to outpatient therapy and cover who would watch our daughter and son. Everyone worked together to help with daunting tasks like getting groceries, taking kids to doctor appointments, caring for the children while I was in court, serving multiple jail sentences, or attending court-ordered treatment.

Logistics had always been a strong point for my husband, so whether he wanted the role of logistics coordinator for our family or not, he was made for it. Getting me to AA meetings was hard at first, because the hours I needed to attend were all through the day and late into the night. We discovered an up-and-coming driving service called Uber that would work for us until I could start building a network at the AA meetings and solicit rides from people.

He also bought me a GED study book so I could study at night when my kids slept. I had mentioned earlier to you that I am a high school dropout. The DUI court program I entered into to avoid prison time required me to obtain my GED. So, we added that to my to-do list... a list that started to resemble one of those CVS receipts that roll out onto the floor and down the hall. But nonetheless, I studied hard, passed the test, and checked it off my list.

My husband continued filling my every hour with constructive things to do until I could find my groove and learn how to function on a day-to-day basis on my own. These were all beautiful gifts he continued to offer me but I almost always faced each one by being agitated and feeling inadequate.

Looking back, I can see exactly what my husband was doing. He was loving me and pushing me forward into sobriety the only way he knew how, one day at a time. Unfortunately for him, this is where the brunt of my choices really started to affect our relationship in the most negative way. His attempts to heal me turned from healthy, loving acts of kindness to a co-dependent relationship like you hear a lot about in recovery—where the "care taker" focuses so much on the "sick person" that they lose themselves in the process. This led to many resentments. I was no longer just a woman in recovery. We had become a family in recovery.

I heard an example that resonated with me at a marriage counseling session. If our family is in a boat and I get up to move, the entire family has to shift themselves to balance the distribution of weight in the boat in order for the boat to not tip over. In my recovery, I had gotten up in the boat to move, but the family was still seated in their original places. So essentially our proverbial recovery boat was tipping and everyone needed to start shifting where they were seated. This would take time—a lot of time and counseling, and I would have to remain patient as things shifted and put my new-found life skills from treatment and AA into action.

Eventually, we survived each looming court date and each week when I would have to check myself into jail to serve a portion of my sentence. We checked the tasks off the spreadsheet as they happened.

In the process, I grew independent and embraced my place in recovery, while my husband was left in a state of feeling unneeded and angry. I would press for him to attend family counseling sessions or Al-Anon meetings and he resisted my suggestions the same way I would when he thought I should get help for drinking.

He never gave up on me in my darkest hours, so I chose to not give up on him. And you know what? With time, eventually things started to shift, and he came around... one day at a time. We are still a work in progress, but as they say in the AA program, "progress not perfection."

Chapter Four

A Spiritual Awakening, Part One

If you know Tom Gissy, then you know what a fine man he was. Our birthdays are four days apart, which makes us both Libras. If you are familiar with astrological signs, then you'll understand we were very similar in the way of a stereotypical Libra. Ruled by our hearts, love, empathy, compassion, and love for nature and the arts keep us charismatically leading in most roles we take on in a way that makes people feel loved and empowered. Forgiving and a strong ability to see all sides of any situation helps us find balance in this crazy universe.

When we are heartbroken or unloved, we become angry and bitter, and overindulge. We root for the underdog even if they have been our enemy. We are often found in the public arena, orchestrating things and sprinkling our charm on anyone we encounter.

We have an ability to connect on a deeper level than some. Because that can be exhausting, we find comfort in retreating occasionally in order to recuperate so we can get back out there in the world and serve where needed, fully and wholeheartedly. My mom always says how much my older sister is like dad, and I agree. As his wife, soulmate, and high school sweetheart, she would be the best judge, I suppose. But those characteristics I just mentioned, those are mine, and it's what connected us with very few words for my entire life.

My sister was always his buddy, and my brother was his only son. But I was his Missy Pooh (Seriously, this was how he introduced me). Most importantly, I was the mother of his only four grandchildren.

He had several songs for me—a made up "Missy Pooh, Missy Pooh, you know what?" Then I would say "What Daddy?" And he would sing... "I think I love you." "Brown Eyed Girl" was another he liked to sing. "Let It Be" by the Beatles was our favorite.

Like him, I was a misunderstood kid, and he constantly snapped at me for my smart mouth. But when I made mistakes, he would be the first to remind me that he knew what it was like to do so. He constantly encouraged me to tap into my faith... that once I did, I would find my purpose and stop exhausting myself with all the nonsense. He rocked me when Bobby Tanner broke my heart, and he chased all over town looking for me when I wandered the streets in danger. He was a "troublemaker" as a teen and had a sibling who was an alcoholic, so he knew what I was walking through before I did. I didn't have to tell him much. He knew my pain.

At the end of his life, he shared things about his own drinking that I wish he would have told me sooner. Why didn't he tell me he knew about my disease at the level he did? He wasn't around long enough to engage with me quite that deep. He was busy—busy being the man that made everyone else love Tom Gissy so much. Don't get me wrong. He would try, and I wouldn't let him in, so he loved me from a distance the best he could.

They say a girl's relationship with her father will impact her relationships with a partner later in life. If that is true, then I can pinpoint where my cat and mouse games came from in all of my relationships. He would cook me something special, pull on my big toe if it was dangling off the side of the couch as he walked through a room, and leave me trinkets in the driver's seat of my car, that were usually related to some inside joke or conversation we had at the time. Private, small comments in my ear or tokens of love were how he decided to love me, and I liked being his center of attention just for the few seconds either one of us would allow before redirecting our attention to other more important things.

He would pop in at any job I had and tell me he happened to be in the neighborhood. And I would act like his visiting me at whatever job I had at the time was no big deal even though my heart could explode that he was proud enough of me to take time from his busy schedule to see me.

I used to tell him, "I'm not really going to know who you are until after you're gone." And I was right. I can't tell you how many people came to me at his funeral to tell me the impact he had on their lives. The things he had done for them, the souls he had awakened, the things he had done for their families—the impact on their faith, recovery, job promotion, marriage, education, or sports. I was so envious with every story that would come to me, at one point I hid in the bathroom just so I didn't have to hear it anymore. I'm sure you are probably thinking I should have been proud. I was, but mostly I was jealous and felt robbed and mad that I never pursued a relationship on my end until I only had a few months left to do so.

He was everywhere all the time, and I suppose now he still is, just in a way we can't see or understand. But rather than continue on with rewriting my father's obituary and try to sell you on what a remarkable man he really was, it is important that I share with you in more depth what I mentioned earlier about the beginning of my spiritual awakening.

Okay, are you ready for this? You may have to read it more than once to really let the magnitude of this sink in. The beginning of my spiritual awakening was watching my father, Tom Gissy, die as I fought to stay alive.

I know... profound, right? But this is the thing that changed my mental thinking, my emotional being, and perspective on life forever. The first entire year of my sobriety was the last year of my dad's life. Sure, I had to get sober and start the necessary steps that would lead me to the moment but that is it. My dad had to die for me to want to live. And the last months of him here on earth saved my life.

In between serving my multiple habitual violator sentences in the Cobb County and Henry County Correction Facilities and attending a rigorous DUI court outpatient program, I got to spend time getting to really know all about the man everyone else knew so well. As part of my sentencing, I lost my right to drive for two years and depended on my dad to shuttle me to court dates, doctor appointments, jail drop-offs, and jail pick-ups.

I could go on and on with the list of places I was required to be with no means to get to said places unless someone could give me a ride. Everyone else had jobs, and he was taking a break from his appraisal business that he had been very successful at after his retirement. He was focused on his chemo treatments, trying to beat stage four pancreatic cancer, but he managed to find time to support my needs.

I finally had him all to myself. Hours of car rides in his red convertible Mustang. Sometimes we just listened to our favorite songs as we enjoyed not having to be anything for anyone for that moment. We were both exhausted, fighting our own battles and trying to stay alive. Some car rides were so deep with conversation we would lose track of where we were headed. He would usually break the ice when I got in his car and say, "Well, let's go... tell me what ya got and where you're at... and go quick... I don't have a lot of time left." He tried to break the ice each time with dark humor, but I always started spilling my guts immediately. Although he "joked" about not having much time left, I was fully aware he was getting sicker day by day, and I wasn't going to waste what time I had left with him.

Shortly after our birthdays, he became ill and never bounced back. Although his first round of chemotherapy gave him much greater results than expected, the cancer was still there spreading like wildfire. He decided to stop the second round of chemo treatments, and hospice stepped in.

In the hospital, he kept giving the same speech over and over to everyone who visited—that when he died it would leave a hole in our hearts, but to not let that hole remain. Rather, plant a rose garden in the hole and care for the roses planted in his honor with love. To not be sad for him because he knew where he was going but to be sad for each other because we would be left behind (for now), and to love each other through it and love one another as Jesus has told us to do. He said, as he lay in the hospital, "Get me well enough so I can go home and get ready to go home."

There are so many moments I can remember vividly about his last days in hospice care, but two stand out above all others. The first is when my Aunt Teresa (his oldest sister) was at the house helping mom sponge-bathe dad and change his sheets. My parents' room makes up the entire right side of the house. On one side is the bedroom and off that is a sitting room that became my dad's hospice care room. I sat on my parents' bed, watching them work together to lift dad and communicate with each other what each step would look like before they did it.

My aunt was a registered nurse and the control coordinator for the University of Georgia Student Health Center. She had several decades of experience caring for others, but this was her baby brother and one of her best friends. My mom had many decades of experience in the healthcare industry as a quality assurance coordinator for Northside Hospital. In our home she was always the caregiver for our family, never afraid to jump in and handle bodily fluids and the science of what is required to get a person well. But this was her husband and her best friend.

I remember thinking, *how can they be going through all the motions with such strength? Aren't they so brave and strong? What is it like to have a sister-in-law that can be by your side to help you change your husband's diaper?* I felt intense love as I watched them work together and talk to dad about each step they were doing next.

I wondered how my dad felt. *Was he embarrassed after being so physically strong for all those years, now laying in his own feces and hoping someone would know he is thirsty and needed his tongue moistened with water? Or was he proud? Proud to have them caring for him and being so kind and respectful to each other through the process. Was he even present? Was he on his way out? Could he see his other sister, Adelle, who had passed away just two years prior from the same disgusting disease on the other side? Were Grandma and Grandpa Gissy there welcoming him home?* I really thought all these things... I remember it vividly to this day.

Before I could ask myself any other questions, my Aunt Teresa looked at me. Her eyes connected to mine, and she said, "Come here, Melissa. We need your help. Your mom is tired, and I'm weak."

I froze. I told her, "No, I can't. I really can't. I don't even know why I am back here honestly... I was just checking to see if..."

She said very firmly, "Yes you can, Melissa, you are stronger than you think. I know you can do this, so come here, and I will tell you what to do."

Before long, I was lifting my dad, straightening his sheets as she sat behind me supervising. I somehow got an adrenaline rush. I was strong enough to lift him, just enough. I think I may have even pushed them out of the way when it was time to change his diaper. I remember saying something like, "I've had kids in diapers, and I can figure this out." I knew you had to wipe in certain directions and how to get the diaper on just right so there wouldn't be any leaks.

I rubbed lotion on his beautiful tan skin. For someone who had been through so much hell physically, his skin was still so soft and healthy. I brushed what hair was left on his head from treatments. I would tell him as I started each grooming technique what I was going to do and for him to make a noise if he didn't like it. As I continued to use my experiences from visiting spas and salons over the years on my dad, he didn't make a sound. He just smiled, and we looked at each other just like we always had... loving each other with few words.

My aunt told me it was time to give him his morphine and to go get it. I paused and looked at her for what felt like eternity. I'm sure it was just a few seconds before I reminded her, I was a drug addict and alcoholic and I probably shouldn't be the one handling the morphine but she instructed me where to get it in the refrigerator and so I did. That was a long walk from the kitchen down the hall back to his death room, holding a drug I had once abused, meant to help my dad through his final hours.

I gave it to my aunt, but she had a hard time deciding how to administer it to him while he was in an almost non-responsive state. I told her I had remembered from my partying days where the liquid should go in your mouth to be most effective. I ended up soaking the tongue-moistening sponge with the liquid morphine and applying it in those spots in my dad's mouth. We could see he instantly received relief.

That would be the first time God granted me an opportunity to use my experience from past mistakes to help someone in need. This transfer from negative energy to positive energy would be the seed planted to show me that the rest of my life could be helping others in some way for good, using lessons from my past. My purpose was set in motion at that very moment. And so began my second half of life, right there at the hour of Tom Gissy's death.

Chapter Five

A Spiritual Awakening, Part Two

I mentioned earlier that there were two situations at the birth of my spiritual awakening. The second one would come just a few days after the morphine experience I shared with you in the previous chapter. Now keep in mind at this point I was a year sober. It was actually the day of my one-year sobriety anniversary. I had come further than I ever had with trying to build a life without alcohol or drugs.

I was in the same room with my father. He slept while I sat in a chair beside him just looking at him, trying to memorize every detail. Family came in and out of the house from all over the country, taking turns sitting with him and making their peace.

My Aunt Teresa arrived at the house and came back to the room. At some point I shared with her that it was my one-year sobriety date. I was supposed to go to an AA meeting to receive the coveted blue chip that marks your sobriety birthday and share my message with fellow alcoholics what that year looked like. There would be people in that room who needed to hear my message because that is the primary purpose in AA... to get sober and share your story with another person who needs to get sober, to be walking-talking beacons of hope for each other.

But my dad was at the hour of his death, and I would not leave his side. The same aunt who had pushed me through physically caring for my dad just days before, now pushed me to leave to go pick up my chip and be there for my sober group. She told me my dad would like to see my blue chip. I told her he hadn't opened his eyes or done anything to respond to us in over twenty-four hours. She insisted I go, and although it was hard to leave my dad's side, off I went.

I'm so grateful I went, because in that meeting, I met my AA sponsor, Lee Lee. It was in that same meeting where I scored the opportunity to complete pending portions of my community service for my DUI court program. It was also in that meeting where I would choose the 8111 AA Clubhouse for my home group. Most importantly, it was in that very meeting that I learned the magnitude of the fourth step and what making amends with people means to your sobriety. This meeting helped me decide that I was not only not drinking anymore, but I was going to pursue a real sober life on a true spiritual level.

When I returned home to Mom and Dad's house, it was quiet. Everyone was in the front living room resting and chatting. I went back to my dad's room. I sat down, and I told him, "Dad, I made it. I made it a year. I'm sober... so now what?" I giggled and placed the blue chip in his hand. He was not responsive but I pulled up a chair and continued to tell him all the wonderful things that transpired at the meeting.

In AA you are supposed to work the twelve steps in order. I completed Step One: "We admitted we were powerless over alcohol-that our lives had become unmanageable" while I was in treatment. I completed Step Two: "Came to believe that a Power greater than ourselves could restore us to sanity" during the first year of my sobriety. Step Three: "Made a decision to turn our will and our lives over to the care of God as we understood Him" came along shortly after my Step Two. To be completely honest with you, God's will, not my will, was hard to exercise. The "one day at a time" thing was tough for me, too, but I was at a place where I had accepted both. In the beginning of my sobriety, I saw nature and the outdoors as my higher power. Eventually, I accepted that my higher power is God.

Steps Four and Five where we "make a fearless moral inventory of ourselves and admit to ourselves, God and another human being the exact nature of our wrongs" is where I had been stuck. My new sponsor, Lee Lee, was going to walk with me through those steps over the next few months, but my dad was dying. There wasn't enough time to prepare with my new sponsor. So, I made a decision to make my first amends with him the best I knew how.

I explained to him how I felt and that I had no idea what I was doing. I asked if he could hear me and if he had the strength, to let me know. There was no response. He was still, peaceful, and quiet, so I journeyed on. I poured my heart out in the most authentic way I could, telling him everything. I told him things I probably should have said years ago. I apologized for any of my actions that may have caused him harm or harm to others whom he loved.

Just at the very end, my mom walked in. She sat down on the other side of him, and we wept together. I told her I didn't think he heard everything I said. We just sat there crying together, petting his hands. And then, he sat forward. He reached for something but we couldn't figure out what. We think it was the picture of Mother Mary behind me although we will never know. He hadn't been responsive for so many hours but he had a sudden burst of energy. He laid back, looked at me, and grunted something I couldn't understand.

I tried to keep calm, but I wanted to shout, "Dad I don't know what you are saying!"

And then he said, "I love you." I looked at my mom, and she confirmed, "Melissa, he said, 'I love you.'"

There it was. My first amends. It was heard and accepted, delivered to him with love and returned to me with love—in the house with a banner that had been hanging my entire life that said, "Love One Another" to a man that has "All you need is love" on his headstone. I had finally seen what love meant in regard to people making mistakes and being forgiven for those mistakes and just loving each other unconditionally.

My dad "went home" as he would say just a few days later. After his body had been carried away, my mom and I went through some of his clothes in his closet. I pulled an index card out of his tuxedo pocket. It was a note written to himself that read, "God is asking me through faith to reach outside myself and love those who may not love me." Written in his own handwriting right before my very eyes was a message to go beyond myself and love people even if they do not reciprocate that love. How profound a concept for an alcoholic who had worn the victim cloak her entire life and had used the excuse to not love because the world did not love her back.

You hear all the time about wonderful legacies that parents leave their children. Some inherit the family farm or take over family businesses. Some are left a car, jewelry, or earthly possessions. Some keep a family recipe going for the next generation. But this one was meant for me, I just felt it. It was my inheritance from him. I was shown that I am to love unconditionally, and in doing so, I was going to have to get to know my higher power, whom I now call God, on a much deeper level. But how? How can an alcoholic deserve to be close to Him? How would I learn to love people even when they don't love me?

I had spent my entire life in the pursuit of being accepted and loved but had never known what love was or really felt like. How could I "love one another" without understanding what love meant? One day at a time... that's how. With God's grace and mercy. And so, the next phase of my spiritual awakening came faster and harder than I was prepared for, but the flood of opportunity to know God was set in motion and I was not turning back under any circumstances.

Chapter Six

Making Moves

Cleaning up the wreckage of your past seems impossible while maneuvering through the beginning stages of sobriety, although I had no choice but to find a way to do both rigorously and painstakingly. Every day I kept a two-part promise to myself—to do the next right thing and to not drink. It started to become clear to me that as long as I stuck to that promise, God would supply a continual flow of aid. I was building the ability to see when I made poor decisions and began taking accountability for my actions.

In recovery they call it "keeping your side of the street clean," and I enjoyed doing just that. It felt good to do the right thing—empowering. My peers in recovery told me I would come to know a new freedom, and they were right. I started to feel the freedom of living a life without a trail of lies and deception following me.

The hardest part about being an honest person after you have lied for so long to yourself and others is that you know you are being honest about your decisions and choices, but your loved ones need time to accept that you are actually capable of being trusted.

The chase for instant gratification drove part of my addiction. And even though I was becoming comfortable living a sober life, I was having a hard time letting go of that part of my ego. I assumed that because I was doing everything expected of me, everyone around me should automatically acknowledge that and accept the new Melissa.

Unfortunately, it didn't work like that. A group counselor from my DUI Court Program, gave me some great advice on how to work through this roadblock. He told me to take the years I had negatively affected my relationships because of my addiction and double that. That's how long it should be before I should expect them to trust me. I'm not sure he meant it literally. His message was more about giving my loved ones time to heal.

It was a bold enough statement that it put me in check. I remembered it every time I would start to feel defeated about my progress not paying off when I thought it should. I began to focus less on my family and friends' acceptance of my progress and focused more on where I could improve myself spiritually or where I could be of service to someone. At times it felt like my past couldn't get behind me fast enough. Regardless, I was making moves and I wasn't slowing down.

As soon as I faced a challenge honestly and thoroughly, I could barely catch my breath before another began. Somehow though, as each challenge arose, I received just what I needed at the perfect time.

At first it was overwhelming how some things would just fall into my lap. Actually, more times than not, they felt like they were getting shoved down my throat. What I understand now as the Holy Spirit working miracles in my life through other people, would almost scare me.

How could someone show up and say just the right thing at just the right time without me even telling them I needed help with that exact thing? God, that's how. He showed me I was on the right path, and as long as I kept Him as my higher power rather than turning to my self-will for direction, He would continue to deliver His grace and mercy.

Now, don't get me wrong. Just because I was getting comfortable with the fact God was in charge didn't mean I knew how to talk to him at this point.

One of the first things I started doing was asking out loud, "God, is that you?" Then I would acknowledge any spiritual gift being sent to me and ask, "What is it that you want me to do with this?"

Most of the time I would feel an answer—a conscious nudge, if you will, that feels similar to the way I heard the voice speak to me that day in my basement. And most of the time I would resist the answer and say things like, "I can't do that" or "I'm not capable." I often asked, "Are you sure that's what you want me to do?" It seems I was always waiting for God to give me an easier task or something that seemed less difficult to accomplish.

Writing this book would be a perfect example of His ongoing patience and guidance to nudge me to do something uncomfortable that I think is beyond my capabilities. But since we are now chapters deep, you can see that after fits of resistance, I eventually listened to Him. Sometimes I question and resist through the entire process, although I keep pushing through the experiences whether I'm fighting everything along the way or not.

Things were starting to feel like a new normal. Without a driver's license, I had to be creative about how to get things done. We found a preschool for my youngest son, which was a little over a mile from my house. I could pack him up in the stroller, drop him off at school, then walk a little further with the stroller to a grocery store that had just been built. I'd shop for groceries until the stroller was packed full, walk back to the house, and do typical stay-at-home parent tasks mixed with my work from home job and assignments for my DUI court program. Later in the day, I walked back to his school and picked him up.

Other parents would see me walking every day, even in the rain and snow, and say, "Wow! You sure are diligent about your exercise. Good for you!"

At first, I would just smile and say, "Thanks," while really I was so embarrassed that I couldn't drive my son to school like a "normal" parent. Eventually, I decided to embrace why I was *getting* to walk rather than *having* to walk.

I shared my story with anyone who crossed my path. They almost always responded with acceptance and often shared their own experiences. I found myself realizing that the statement I heard back in rehab—that I will never have to feel alone ever again—was starting to make sense.

You see, I was only alone with my disease when I hid behind my guilt and shame. As soon as I found the courage to begin embracing my disease and sharing my journey with others, I found that just about anyone I shared it with either dealt with alcoholism themselves or knew of someone who has.

A recent study from the World Health Organization shows that a staggering number of 240 million people worldwide struggle with alcoholism. And I'm sure that number doesn't include the people still sitting in quiet isolation thinking they are alone. So, you see, by sharing my story with other people, I embraced my disease and found acceptance with it.

Lots of responsibilities packed each day, but we seemed to make even the most hectic times work. I remember when I would start getting overwhelmed or anxious, gratitude would immediately take over. That was not a normal way of thinking for me. I had been a victim for so long that this newly learned ability to see light within the darkness kept me in awe and allowed me to enjoy the pink cloud of recovery I mentioned in a previous chapter that I thought I was not going to get. This included simple thoughts of thanking God for the stroller and nice walking shoes rather than having anxiety over not having a car. I expressed gratitude for the opportunity to enjoy nature all around me while walking when most people zipped by in their cars. I was getting to take everything in around me each day, hearing birds sing, and enjoying the different smells each new season brought with it.

I was starting to make a sober friend network and moving rapidly through the twelve-step program. My marriage was still very strained from all the havoc I had caused, and my relationship with my children was far from repaired, but we were all still intact with many bandages (maybe even duct tape) holding us together. That was good enough for me at the time.

I eventually graduated from the DUI court program. I wasn't out of the water yet… just still doggy paddling hard enough to keep my head above water when we found out my father-in-law who lived in North Carolina was diagnosed with Alzheimer's.

We moved to North Carolina and used the opportunity for my husband to be there for his father and family as they maneuvered through my father-in-law's terminal disease. This experience gave us a fresh start.

In what felt like an overnight decision for my husband and me, we packed and off to North Carolina we went, not knowing where we would land. We had no long-term plan of action in place. We just knew we were making moves and we were doing it together.

Chapter Seven

Welcome Home

People in North Carolina say "bless your heart" a lot. I was never really sure if they were truly blessing my heart or if they were blessing me off. Either way, I decided I was going to take it as meaning my heart was being blessed. After all, I needed all the blessings I could get. Relocating to a new state with no family and friends, no sober network, and an immediate family that was still mad at me all the time was very difficult and extremely lonely.

I thought to myself several times, *"I have made a big mistake. This is when I'm going to drink again, I'm sure of it."* But I didn't. Take one guess at what happened. That's right, God showed up once again and did for me what I could not do for myself. And this one was a life changer.

After a temporary stay with my mother-in-law, we found a rental home. My husband had started his new job, the kids were off at their new schools. I sat in a half-unpacked house all alone, and I lost it. I panicked. I just knew I had made one

• • •
- 77 -

of the biggest mistakes in my new sober life by agreeing to move to North Carolina.

I packed my bags as fast as I could, got in the car, and I was ready to run back to Georgia, permanently. I was driving down the road, talking to my husband on the phone, telling him I had made a mistake by moving and that I couldn't stay. He was trying his best while at work to calm me down and asked where I was. I had been driving in circles for over an hour. He told me to pull over, to look around, and tell him where I was.

I pulled into a parking lot just short of the highway I had spent the last hour searching for, and looked up to see a sign that said Holy Family Catholic Church. I was speechless. I felt goosebumps all over my body. I saw my reflection in my rear-view mirror, and I remember the terrified look on my face as if I had seen a ghost.

After a long pause, I calmly told my husband that I would head back to our rental home and explain to him later, when he got home from work, what had changed my mind about running away. I call it running away because that's what I had always done. Even sober, I was still trying to run when things got too overwhelming. But not this time, God had different plans for me.

I need to back up a little bit to share with you some important details about why pulling into that church parking lot and seeing that sign was enough to quiet me and send me home. Just a few days prior to that freak-out episode, my husband had mentioned to me there was a Catholic church I should call where I could complete my community service hours.

I mentioned in chapter six that I had graduated the DUI court program prior to moving, but I didn't mention this very important piece. Because I had multiple DUIs in several counties in Georgia, the Cobb County DUI Court Program had merged all of my cases into one county to serve my sentences consecutively, which included hundreds of hours of Community Service. With all the transfers in paperwork, they somehow overlooked two-hundred forty hours that were still due. I got a call from my probation officer that I had a limited amount of time to get them finished and I had permission to complete them in North Carolina since I had already relocated and transferred my probation there.

You would think this would have caused me turmoil, believing that I had graduated the DUI Court Program by completing all my required tasks to later find out that wasn't the case, but it didn't.

I remember when I received the phone call how upset everyone was. My family kept asking me if I was in shock and how could I be in such a calm state. I remember an overwhelming feeling of acceptance and again, I heard that voice from within speaking to me. It was telling me all will be well and this was meant to be. They call this acceptance, and I was starting to practice it with ease.

I shared with my family that I believed this was happening for a reason. I couldn't explain it but I knew it was meant to be this way. I shared the idea that it will be a way for me to make a new sober connection in North Carolina. You see, this small "set back" was a blessing in disguise. A blessing that led me to writing the this very book and connecting me to you through these pages.

I had my mind set on a food pantry near our house to volunteer at, but my husband was pushing for me to call the church. The Catholic Church where I spent my entire childhood and young adult life was also named Holy Family Catholic Church. It was the church where all of my spiritual seeds were planted, where my sacraments were made, and where my four children had been baptized. Holy Family was the church where my dad was a sponsor to my husband to become a Catholic. It is where I attended my grandparents and dad's funeral services. It was the church where I met my dad in the parking lot, in tears, wasted, begging to be taken back to rehab for my final attempt at sobriety. The name Holy Family Catholic Church was woven into every fiber of my being from the very first years of my life.

Now, when I wanted to run away from everything and contemplated a relapse, begging God to show me a sign of what to do, I looked up and literally saw a sign that said Holy Family Catholic Church. How could this be? How could I be in a new town, three hundred miles away from what I knew as home, and that's where I parked my car to calm down? That was also the church my husband prompted me to call for community service hours. I believe God was showing me not to run away—that I was exactly where He wanted me to be.

The next morning, I called the church to see if I could do my community service there. Shaking, I made myself tell the lady who answered the phone about my situation. Although nervous, I had to go through with this... the options were complete my hours or go back to jail. I blurted out my story, enough of it to get my foot in the door anyway. After talking for a bit, she shared that they were getting ready to start a parish mission and they were still working on a name for it. She felt like I could probably complete some of my service hours assisting them with setting up for it.

Once our phone call ended, I felt that same nudge I have mentioned to you before. You know that voice I heard but it was more like a feeling rather than hearing it with my ears. It was telling me to call the lady back and suggest a name for the mission. The name for the mission I heard in my head was "Better Things Are Coming."

I don't remember how the phone call went exactly. I was too preoccupied thinking about how the woman I spoke with must think I'm crazy. She didn't treat me like I was crazy at all though. She seemed grateful for my suggestion and told me she would pass it on. Shortly after that, I was in touch with the faith formation director in charge of screening volunteers. And within a week or two I reported for duty, willing to do whatever I was asked.

One day while working on my community service hours, I walked by the office of the lady I spoke with on the phone. She called out to me and said, "Guess what, Missy, they named the parish mission Better Things Are Coming!" I was completely shocked. I felt like I didn't have a voice for many years, so I couldn't believe someone actually liked my idea. My feelings of accomplishment for the first few years in sobriety were all related to recovery, so it felt amazing to be part of something outside of that.

Moving forward, I'll refer to the lady I keep mentioning as Vicki. I haven't used many names while sharing my story, but Vicki, much like the people mentioned in the introduction, has been a driving force in my writing this book. I think it only makes sense that I call her by her name as she plays such an important role in who I am today.

You see, she didn't just take part in encouraging me to share my story with you, she also is my mentor. She is a thin lady with a petite bone structure, but don't let that fool you. She is from New Jersey and has no problem telling you like it is. She is tough. But her heart is one of the most generous and softest I have ever known. She is a Libra just like me and my dad. Sometimes we don't even have to say a word to each other, and we already know what the other thinks or feels.

In our relationship, her expectation is that I'm constantly pushing myself to grow in different areas of my life. This means sometimes I'm really mad at her. I love her but she makes me do the work that requires me to be the best I can be, and that's not always easy.

Having a mentor doesn't always mean you are best friends. You need someone whom you can trust that they are being honest with you and guiding you along your life's journey with the right intentions. She is the first person in my life who helped me truly believe that people make mistakes, and that it is okay. She isn't afraid to ask me the tough questions and expects authentic answers. Most often, I have to think on things for days before I can come back to her with my responses, and she is okay with that. She doesn't put time limits on my growth. She is patient with me. And when I receive positive feedback, I know it's well-earned.

When I left Georgia, I left behind my AA sponsor, Lee-Lee. She was a tough cookie. She was exactly what I needed to get me through those first few years of sobriety. She has a story of her own, and her experiences with recovery guided me through some of the hardest first steps in my sobriety. In the AA program, a sponsor is a mentor or a guide who has been in recovery and worked the twelve steps. Finding a mentor whether you are in the AA program or using other avenues to find your sobriety is important, especially in the beginning.

When I first moved to North Carolina, I still checked in with my sponsor, Lee Lee. But I knew almost instantly when I met Vicki that God had placed her in my life to support the shift in direction that was happening in my recovery. I was focusing more on self-exploration and developing an understanding of faith and religion. Vicki led me to a counselor, who would eventually lead to marriage counseling for my husband and me. I had no doubt that all of the wonderful things that were finally starting to fall into place were direct gifts from God. His placing two women like Lee Lee and Vicki in my life were some of my greatest blessings to remind me that I was not alone.

After several weeks of community service work at the church, my hours were almost complete. In that short time, I was beginning to know the staff and even some parishioners. After they found out I had office experience, they moved me from some of the more labor intense duties to clerical work. I sat in a small cubical away from everyone in the back of a worship center. I was surrounded by the familiar childhood smells from church. It was even built the same year as the Holy Family in Georgia so the aesthetics were almost identical.

I felt like I had purpose every day. I would drop off my son at school and go sit in my little cubical, working as hard and as fast as I could. The staff would come peek around the cubical wall and chat for a minute. I would try my best to interact, but I was so socially awkward.

I had been sober for a few years but I hadn't had much interaction with people outside my small recovery bubble. This is where my friendship with Father Peter began. On his way to his office from mass every morning, he would check in on me. It was after many of our morning chats and listening to pieces of my story that he started planting the seed I should write a book.

As time went by, I gained confidence and even made friends outside of work. As I grew spiritually, all other aspects of my life improved.

One day, I was sharing with Vicki that my community service hours were complete. I asked if I could please continue to volunteer. I knew being there every day for a few hours was orchestrated by God. He had placed me within His walls to keep me safe and surround me with so many people who had a great wealth of knowledge about His love. I did not know how to continue my daily presence there once my hours were finished. But He heard my prayers at night, and He had my new mentor offer me a part-time job. I would have stayed for free, but Vicki and the pastor at the time believed I was worth investing in... and so began my permanent place in the Holy Family Church family. And it really felt like family. My co-workers and parishioners became my brothers and sisters. I was so connected to some of them, it felt like I had known them my entire life. And for the first time in decades, I felt like I was home.

Chapter Eight

Fall Seven Times, Get Up Eight

About a year or so into my most recent attempt at sobriety, I was riding in the car with my mom to one of my many counseling appointments. We were having a conversation about my recovery and what things would look like in my future as far as ongoing counseling was concerned. In that conversation, I mentioned that I would always be an addict.

I thought she understood how my addiction was a disease, but I quickly learned I was mistaken. I explained that my entire life would be an ongoing task to live differently. I told her that she wasn't going to be able to kiss my "boo boo" and place a bandage on it...this healing process was going to be between me and God, and support from her was critical.

My mom is a perfectionist of sorts with a very black and white personality. If there is a problem, you fix it. And if it can't be fixed, then you sweep it under the rug—make it go away and move on. There would be no more sweeping things under the rug in regard to my addictions.

I told her that alcoholism doesn't get "fixed." It just doesn't work like that. She was devastated. I remember vividly, we were at a stop light, and the cars behind us began honking because the light had turned green, but she was too busy fighting back tears to recognize it. She thought a person could get sober and then everything would be "normal."

She asked me, in a very frantic state, "Why did we go through all of this trouble if you are able to drink again and die? What is the point of all this?"

I had to remain calm and remind her that's what all the hard work was for, to know how to live life without needing to ever drink or drug. The encouraging words that flowed out of my mouth did not match the feelings brewing inside of me. I immediately reverted back to the days when I was an utter disappointment to her. I felt defensive, defeated, and ashamed. There was complete silence for the remainder of the fifteen-minute drive, which actually felt like an hour.

When we arrived at our destination, I got out of the car and darted to the closest bathroom. I locked myself in a stall and sobbed, feeling like a complete waste. All of my thoughts of being a failure and a burden to people I loved, boiled inside me no matter how hard I tried to suppress them. My mind raced as I sat in the bathroom. I wanted to drink on those feelings. I began obsessing about where I could get a hold of something, anything that could make me numb. As I sat there in the bathroom stall, wrestling between the urge to drink and prayers for serenity, my counselor knocked on the door and invited me to join them for our meeting.

I didn't have the opportunity to drink in that particular scenario. We would be able to continue the conversation from our car ride in a   safe place with a counselor who was educated on this type of family in recovery scenario. I can only imagine, if things didn't line up the way they did, what I may have chosen to do in order to cope with the feelings of disappointment and worthlessness that came about during our conversation in the car that day. I'm sharing this moment in my journey with you because this is a perfect example of how relapse can take place. The definition of relapse is a recurrence of a past condition.

People tend to believe recovery is permanent once it is achieved, but the truth is that relapse, at some point, will inevitably become a part of your journey. It is a word you should get familiar with and embrace, so you can be prepared when it tries to rear its ugly head.

I have come to know three stages of relapse in my addiction. The first stage is *emotional relapse*. This is when you are not necessarily thinking about using substances, though your actions and behavior may start paving the path to do so. You have triggers that are usually initiated by stress, which can cause anger, anxiety, and depression, changes in self-care like sleeping or eating habits, feelings of loneliness, isolation, frustration, irritability, and mood swings. If your emotions or triggers are not addressed, they can start playing tricks on your way of thinking.

Imagine the scenario you may have seen in comics or cartoons with an angel on one shoulder whispering good advice and a devil on the other shoulder feeding lies and deception, with the character in the middle trying to decipher which one to listen to. This is where ongoing counseling, sober networks, and the DUI Court second chance program stepped in for me in my first few years of sobriety, to hold me accountable, until I could get to a place where I would recognize my warning signs.

It is a common practice in the recovery community to use the word HALT. This word reminds you to pause before you take action. It gives you a chance to ask yourself am I **H**ungry, **A**ngry, **L**onely, **T**ired? This is something I clung tight to in my first years. It was a quick way for me to pause and identify where some of my triggers came from. I still use it to this very day.

Each person's path to recovery is their own. Learning what your warning signs are is crucial in maintaining your sobriety. If they are avoided, it will inevitably lead to the next stage of relapse referred to as *mental relapse*.

During a mental relapse, you may start to feel strange in your own skin. Your underlying emotions may create a mental conflict, and you become disconnected. You find yourself contemplating using substances again. These thoughts will come and go.

In this stage, I would romanticize about drinking or using drugs, but I could quickly remind myself of the turmoil that doing so caused me and everyone I loved. This banter in your mind, while the rest of the world is going on around you, leads to complacency in your sobriety and fuels the obsession of your disease slowly over time. If you stay in that stage long enough without getting the help you need to bounce back, your "addictive brain" will become stimulated, which will increase triggers and cravings. This is when I would find myself skipping therapy appointments and not talking about my feelings with my loved ones and support network. I would excuse myself from much of the work that was needed to keep me sober.

My addictive brain would tell me, "You are fine Melissa, you've got this. You don't need help. Don't tell anyone you are feeling the way you do. It will just cause concern for everyone. There is nothing to be worried about. I mean you're not actually drinking, right?"

My addictive brain was right about one thing, I wasn't drinking yet. But if I stayed in a mental relapse long enough, trying to resolve things on my own will, I would eventually find myself in the third stage, which is *physical relapse*.

This is the hardest stage to bounce back from because this is where you are actually drinking or using drugs again. Once you take that first drink, you will believe that you cannot return to sobriety because the shame, guilt, hopelessness, and disappointment will take over and consume you. This kind of thinking led me to weeks, maybe months of binge drinking and trying to hide or cover up that I had "fallen off the wagon." This stage in relapse is what led me to the cold hard floor of my basement where I tried to take my own life.

You are not the only one who will walk through different stages of relapse. Everyone relapses from something at some point. Maybe you are reading this and you aren't the one struggling with addiction. Maybe you are the one who is trying to understand why someone you love would work so hard at getting sober, just to throw it all away. You have the ability to find empathy and compassion for the addict if you take a moment to consider that you have most likely relapsed in areas of your own life.

Think about times you have backed away from a fitness regimen, or maybe stopped taking medications you know you need to keep you healthy. Maybe you have relapsed in your faith or in your career. You can think about the times in your life where you have worked diligently at something, only to find yourself complacent and off track. Did you get back on track? Maybe you found another route or means of support for what you were trying to accomplish.

Looking inward at your own life scenarios may not help you fully understand what the addict is walking through, but it will help you relate in a way that can give you words of encouragement to the addict to get back up, to keep trying. Relating to someone who is at their bottom and offering support through your own experiences is the best way to connect and show them that they are not alone, they are loved, and they can recover.

The opposite of addiction is connection, which is very much what an addict needs to keep moving forward. Al-Anon is a wonderful support system for people learning how to balance healthy boundaries, while finding ways to love someone through their recovery from addiction.

Fall seven times, get up eight is an age-old proverb that essentially means it doesn't matter how many times you fall, as long as the number of times you get back up is greater than the number of times you have fallen. I have made several attempts at getting sober. I "fell" seven times by choosing to drink in my sobriety. I have relapsed many times in all three stages. But I got back up. If I hadn't, I wouldn't be here today writing to you. I would have missed all of the beautiful things that have come on this eighth attempt at a new way of life.

* * *

You can look at relapse one of two ways. You can see it as failure and use it as your excuse to take you straight down the path that leads to jails, institutions, and death. Or you can find humility and gratitude in the things that relapse brings and get back on the path of sobriety.

I discovered empathy, and my ability to feel compassion grew with each time I had to get up and try again. In fact, I found my purpose in advocating for people with addiction during the upswing from one of my longest, darkest relapse periods.

Sobriety is hard work, for both the person in recovery and their loved ones. The thought of all that progress and hope being in vain can be devastating to everyone involved. Anyone can stop drinking, but to get sober and remain sober takes work, support, and the understanding of how to stay proactive instead of reactive in a relapse.

Once you recognize your triggers in stage one of relapse, this will be your game changer. You will begin to recognize where you are headed and do things that work for you to get back on track. And if you do happen to take that drink, all is not lost.

You have a community of millions of alcoholics worldwide who have been where you are and believe in you. Stay connected, know your warning signs, act on them when you recognize them, allow your support network to help hold you accountable, and most importantly, always remember to do all of these things one day at a time.

Chapter Nine

Breaking the Stigma

Right now, as I am writing to you, we are smack in the middle of the COVID-19 Pandemic. There is so much talk of the pandemic that you hardly ever hear of the drug and alcohol epidemic also going on worldwide. As I mentioned in Chapter Seven, I work in a church so burying people is a part of the business. You would be shocked to know that many of the funerals recently weren't COVID-related at all. They were people dying from addiction... young lives lost way too soon.

Every time we received news of another life lost, I would be reminded almost immediately how writing this book for you wasn't just an "I'll get to it when I can..." task on my lengthy to-do list. It was a personal responsibility, and even more so, a privilege. My heart broke with every devastated family member who had to make that phone call to us in preparation for their loved one's funeral—the one who wasn't getting the second chance I had gotten. For them it was too late. But it's not for you and me.

I couldn't call this book complete without addressing this current crisis and making an honest effort to break the stigma about addiction. The phrase "addiction is a choice, not a disease" is my least favorite thing to hear someone say. There are a lot of close runners-up in respect to statements about the disease of addiction, but the number one spot goes to that phrase I just mentioned, which basically implies that addiction is chosen by the addict.

It is understandable how people with little knowledge about addiction can think like that. I mean, I chose to go run around town with the wrong crowd, right? I chose to experiment with drugs and drink the vodka using my fake ID, right? I chose to eat my Xanax like candy instead of taking it as prescribed, right? The answer to all of those questions is yes. Those are all true statements. I did make those choices. But once I made those choices consistently, my drinking became a disease. This happened over time because I needed more and more drugs and alcohol to achieve the same level of pleasure from when I first began drinking. My tolerance level increased as my satisfaction level decreased, creating the chase referred to in recovery as "the obsession."

Here is the best example I can think of to explain how telling someone they chose to be an alcoholic is a stigma rather than a fact. When someone gets Type 2 diabetes from being overweight, it is still a disease right? The person with diabetes chose to live an unhealthy lifestyle, so they now have diabetes, which is a disease.

Once you are diagnosed with diabetes, your doctor comes up with a plan to manage it, correct? Maybe you exercise more, change your diet, get on a form of insulin, and maybe even join some support groups or buy literature to help you become more informed about your new diagnosis. You build a network of other people who have the same issue, and you work out together or chat online about meal planning and better habits. You may even seek a life coach to help you stay accountable for your actions.

This is the same exact road map for the addiction recovery path. You chose to take the drink or pop the pill, but at some point, it becomes addiction. Once you admit you have an addiction and are ready to get help, you take similar steps as the person with diabetes might take when they are first diagnosed. Similarly, you come up with a treatment plan, change your diet (starting with eliminating drugs and/or alcohol), and try exercise, yoga and meditation. Maybe you will be prescribed some medications, find a support group, and buy literature to inform you and your loved ones about your recovery. You may find a life coach (in AA they are called sponsors) who can help you hold yourself accountable.

I gave you the example of diabetes, but you could look at other diseases like skin cancer or lung cancer as well. You chose to overexpose yourself to the sun and did not use proper sun protection, but you did not choose skin cancer, it is a disease. You chose to smoke cigarettes or a pipe, but you did not choose to have lung cancer, it is a disease. Alcoholics choose to drink, but those personal choices led to a disease.

I am sure my writing is starting to seem redundant, but my purpose of saying it over and over with different scenarios is to make sure you understand by the time you finish reading this chapter that you do not choose to be an alcoholic. It is imperative for you to know and accept the stigma that you choose to be an addict is a lie. This lie will perpetuate your shame and guilt, keeping you from a successful recovery, mark my words.

Choice does NOT determine whether something is a disease. A disease is what happens as a result of choices. If someone tells you differently, they are welcome to take up their argument with the American Medical Association.

Addiction is defined by the American Medical Association as follows: *Addiction is a treatable, chronic medical disease involving complex interactions among brain circuits, genetics, the environment, and an individual's life experiences. People with addiction use substance or engage in behaviors that become compulsive and often continue despite harmful consequences.*

In short, you are an addict based on a combination of biological psychological, and environmental factors. Once the brain has been changed by addiction, experts believe the person loses control over their behavior. Genetic risk factors and family history play a huge role. In fact, genetics account for over a fifty percent chance of likelihood that someone will become an addict.

Addiction is a chronic disease, *not* a moral issue. So, if you are telling yourself that you are worthless because you are an alcoholic or addict, then please stop. You have a disease. You are just sick. That's it. And the good news is, it is treatable, and you can and will recover. I am living proof. And like me, you will see the twelve promises of Alcoholics Anonymous become a reality for you when you continue to do the next right thing, one day at a time.

When I began writing *I'm Sober...So Now What?* over two years ago, I honestly didn't know the answer to what the "now what" was. You see, I had become so accustomed to my new way of life by checking off the to-do lists and focusing on trying to stay in the moment that I hadn't realized the "so now what" included embracing my second half of life, sober. It became clear to me through writing to you that I had been taking my opportunity at a second chance at life and using it to live every day to the fullest, despite what I may have be dealing with at any given time.

I can't tell you what your "now what" will be. You get to make that decision. Your story will be written by you. Each day will be a new page, each season a new chapter. And at some point, somehow, some way, your recovery story will help another person who needs to know it can be done. That's how it works. We recover and then inspire hope in others who need it.

I believe in you. And until we meet again, may God grant you the serenity to accept the things that you cannot change, the courage to change the things that you can, and the wisdom to know the difference.

Chapter Ten

God...Can You Hear Me?

When I started walking my path to sobriety, I had no idea how to talk to God. I felt awkward and wasn't sure if I was doing it right, almost like when I am at the beginning stages of dating someone. That sounds silly I know but if you think about it, you are building a relationship with Him, so feeling awkward as you maneuver through how you will communicate with Him isn't that silly at all.

Some of my deepest, most authentic talks have been in places in which you wouldn't think God could hear me—the closet in my bedroom, the car driving to work, the shower, sitting in a fast-food drive through, sitting at my desk, and while I'm cooking. My point is you can talk to him anytime, and whether you are speaking out loud or thinking to yourself, I can assure you that He hears our innermost thoughts and desires.

I used to say out loud, "God... can you hear me?" I would awkwardly introduce myself as if He didn't already know me. I eventually learned over time that there is no wrong way to talk to God. I certainly don't feel the need to introduce myself anymore. I prefer most times to say prayers out loud for fear I am not being heard. That's my middle child syndrome showing itself, I suppose.

Early on in my sobriety, I picked a few prayers that spoke to me and made it a practice to say them at different times throughout the day. I set reminders at first, but eventually, it became part of my daily routine.

For example, when I wake up, before my feet even hit the floor, I say my morning prayer. Before I eat lunch, I say the Lord's Prayer. Essentially, I picked a time throughout the day and attached a prayer to that recurring event so I wouldn't forget. I have found that having them with me throughout my day keeps me grounded. They remind me to take a brief time-out from whatever I am doing to reset and make sure I am still connected to my higher power rather than making my way through the day on my own will and ego.

I hope that some of these prayers that have brought me through my "one day at a time" will also bring peace and comfort to you.

Serenity Prayer

God, grant me the serenity to accept the things I cannot change, the courage to change the things I can, and the wisdom to know the difference. Amen.

The Lord's Prayer

Our Father, Who art in heaven, hallowed be Thy name; Thy kingdom come; Thy will be done on earth as it is in heaven. Give us this day our daily bread; and forgive us our trespasses as we forgive those who trespass against us; and lead us not into temptation but deliver us from evil. Amen.

Guardian Angel Prayer

Angel of God, my guardian dear, to Whom His love commits me here. Ever this day be at my side to light and guard to rule and guide. Amen.

Third Step Prayer

God, I offer myself to Thee. To build with me & to do with me as Thou wilt. Relieve me of the bondage of self, that I may better do Thy will. Take away my difficulties, that victory over them may bear witness to those I would help of Thy Power, Thy love & Thy way of life, may I do Thy will always. Amen.

The Fiat of the Eternal Father
(Morning Prayer)

My beloved Father, thy will be done on Earth as it is in Heaven. Be thou my Father. Be always my Eternal Father. Do not leave my soul. Do not abandon me. Do not leave me out of your sight, my Father, for I am your child whom you have created to please you, to adore You, to honor You, living my days as You have given me the license to live it. Amen.

Prayer for Daily Neglects
(Evening Prayer)

My God, who unceasingly calls us to union with You, I ask You to pardon my daily neglects when I ignored and rejected this call and to make me love You more, so that I never miss Your offer to grow in holiness. Amen.

Hail Mary

Hail Mary, Full of Grace, The Lord is with thee. Blessed are thou among women, and blessed is the fruit of thy womb, Jesus. Holy Mary, Mother of God, pray for us sinners now, and at the hour of death. Amen.

The Unity Prayer

My adorable Jesus, may our feet journey together.
May our hands gather in unity.
May our hearts beat in unison.
May our souls be in harmony.
May our thoughts be as one.
May our ears listen to the silence together.
May our glances profoundly penetrate each other.
May our lips pray together to gain mercy
from the Eternal Father. Amen.

Prayer for Hope and Healing

God, you are our source of hope and healing.
In You, there is calm and the only true peace in the universe.
Grant to each of us an awareness of your presence, and give
us perfect confidence in You. In all pain, weariness
and anxiety, teach us to yield ourselves to your never-failing
care, knowing that your love and presence surrounds us,
trusting in your wisdom to give us hope, healing, serenity
and peace in your perfect timing. Amen.

Chapter Eleven

Note to Self

Over the years I have been encouraged to put my thoughts into writing. I was always resistant to the suggestion of placing what was on my mind onto paper. I would try but never with much effort.

To be completely honest, journaling sounded boring and maybe even scary. I would think, *why would I want to write things down that could be found and possibly used against me?* You have to remember; I was an addict for a long period of my life. All of my thoughts, secrets, guilt, and shame were to be tucked away or masked, not written about.

I believe my resistance to try journaling really was about fear of not being ready to connect with my reality. I clung to my denial, and in an extremely dysfunctional way, I protected myself from feeling the things I needed to feel.

I felt crippled by fear that I wasn't smart enough to write anything. I would try and then tell myself, "You aren't doing this right." Then I would either crumble the page or tuck my notebook away in a sock drawer so I didn't have to look at it anymore. But the suggestion always came back up that I should try journaling. And so, the cycle of not really trying and then talking myself out of it would begin again... and again... and again for several years.

When I started in-patient treatment for my addictions, journaling became an assignment, homework if you will. I was required to write just a few thoughts each night to share with my treatment counselors. The task was daunting, but I did each assignment as instructed. At this point in my life, I was finally ready to do whatever it took to heal. Yes, I even submitted to writing.

And you know what? I quickly found that it wasn't as scary or as overwhelming as I had imagined. I saw almost instantly that writing just a few jumbled thoughts could open a window of dialogue with myself. It helped me identify things I could share with my counselors, in my group sessions and recovery meetings. And when I shared those few thoughts in my safe places, it led to discussions that not only helped me process those thoughts, but it helped others process theirs as well.

By opening a window to my mind through journaling, a window to my soul was being opened simultaneously. And that touched the souls of others. Witnessing this transfer of love caught my attention and is where I found my motivation to keep going, to keep journaling. It started with a pen and scratch piece of paper that said, "Note to Self."

You may have heard or read about how the little things add up to big things. Baby steps can make the biggest impact on your life. This is one of those baby steps you can take that could lead to bigger things. For example, look at my story—the woman who didn't have time for some silly idea of journaling has now written a book to share hope with you!

I've shared how journaling helped me, but there are many other ways it has strengthened my life. Here are a just a few examples for you to consider:

- Provides a way to focus on goals
- Helps identify triggers
- Tracks progress and growth
- Improves self-confidence
- Lessons feelings of anxiety and reduces stress
- Brings inspiration
- Encourages self-love
- Eliminates negative self-talk
- Initiates growth toward emotional awareness

I believe strongly in the idea that connection is the opposite of addiction. I had to eliminate the substance use, connect with others, and most importantly, connect with myself. That last sentence, although a short one, lists three essential elements of recovery. None of it is easy...we aren't promised an easy. What we are promised in recovery is that with consistency and honest effort, we will find a better way of life.

Perhaps the first steps to that better way of life for you could include a pen and a few pages of paper to jot down some thoughts. I've added some pages in this book for you to give it a try. They are titled the same way as mine when starting out—Note to Self.

Start small. Maybe something from this book stood out that you can relate to? Write it down and open that proverbial window I just mentioned. Perhaps you prefer expressing yourself with drawing? It doesn't have to be perfect – use stick figures if necessary. I am always reminding myself "progress *not* perfection". This is a grace I give to myself, when trying something new. It encourages me to focus on smaller achievements instead of the end goal.

The point is to put pen to paper and see what comes from within. While you are bravely giving it a try, whether it's in print, cursive, shorthand, spelled correctly or not, remember, you are not alone.

I'm most likely sitting somewhere in this world doing the same thing, thinking of you—praying for your courage and strength—one day at a time.

Note to Self:

_____

_____

_____

_____

_____

_____

_____

_____

_____

_____

_____

_____

_____

_____

You are taking the first steps in healing! Keep going!

Note to Self:

_____

_____

_____

_____

_____

_____

_____

_____

_____

_____

_____

_____

The window is opening! Keep going – I am proud of you!

Note to Self:

If you get stuck, write down a few things that you are grateful for.

Note to Self:

This space is safe - express emotions without worry of being judged.

Note to Self:

_____

_____

_____

_____

_____

_____

_____

_____

_____

_____

_____

_____

_____

_____

These thoughts are helping you process emotions. You're doing it!

Note to Self:

List things you would like to discover on your recovery path.

Note to Self:

_____

_____

_____

_____

_____

_____

_____

_____

_____

_____

_____

_____

_____

Life on life's terms can hit hard sometimes. Let it out.

Chapter Twelve

Podcasts & Online Connections

Right now, we are fortunate to either be in recovery or just beginning to look at the possibilities that ditching the drink or drug might bring us. No matter if we are just starting out, or we have been on the recovery path for years, there is a movement of social justice for breaking the stigma of addiction, and you and I my friend are right in the middle of it.

The days of secret meetings, code words for 12-step programs and anonymity are shifting. You may hear the argument from people with long-term sobriety, that recovering behind closed doors worked for them for decades –why altar the process?

There are several reasons for the shift. A few main factors come to the forefront each time I dive into this complex, worldwide transition. Simply put, the social impacts from Covid-19 left millions of people yearning to have a voice, and technology has made having that voice possible. With suicide and overdose rates at an all-time high, people are uniting across the globe to bring awareness. In a few short years, this has created a recovery world unlike anything we have ever witnessed before.

Today's technology allows information at lightning speeds. Social media may have its draw backs in some areas, but for the intent and purpose of its design for connecting people, recovery from addiction has been planted within it and is blooming exponentially.

Recovery pages on social media offer connection with a reach far greater than what we may find with in-person group meetings. Some of my closest friends in recovery were found online and through social networking. Please do not misunderstand my message. I couldn't imagine my recovery path without "the rooms". If you are new to recovery, this is lingo for actively participating in a recovery program such as Alcoholics Anonymous. These rooms I mention have played a very important role in my recovery and could for you too.

My point is to share that in my experience, I have found that having a balance of both in-person meetings and online connections can be very beneficial. The options for unity on these social pages are endless and offer connections to people you wouldn't be able to meet locally.

My social page, Sober-Now, delivers inspirational messages and connections to other pages for live events and podcasts. Podcasts are an excellent resource for many in recovery from addiction. Usually posted on a weekly or monthly basis, these online radio-like conversations can be accessed from home, while in the car, taking a walk or anywhere you have time to listen.

Most podcasters post their content across several different platforms, allowing the option to also view the podcast either live streamed or prerecorded. Several recovery-related podcasts are hosted by people who have experienced addiction firsthand. These podcasters share impactful information and the valuable lessons they have learned along their journey through recovery. Many podcasters provide their listeners the opportunity to be a guest and share their stories, offering hope, and inspiration to others.

I cannot begin to count the times in early sobriety that I needed to hit a meeting but so often my need would rear its head when none were available. Today, when I feel the urge for connection and can't attend a meeting, I can use my phone or laptop and find a podcast to help me process whatever emotion I am experiencing with my recovery. I simply scroll through the topics and descriptions until I discover one that is specific to my needs.

I find great inspiration in the thousands of episodes that are available to us at any given time, thanks to the rigorous hours of work podcasters spend on creating these programs, as well as the brave individuals who recover out loud by sharing their testimony.

Listed in the next few pages, are some of the recovery-related podcasts that I have found to be beneficial to my daily life. Each of these podcasts have several episodes available online and are accessible to anyone at any time. I have even included a sober book club and a sober library, in case you are interested in staying up to date with some of the best recovery books out there.

When this book originally launched in May of 2022, I was extremely fortunate to connect with several of these platforms to share my message of hope. The opportunity to spend time with them has created connections world-wide. I encourage you to give them a try and who knows... you may even find a few episodes where I am guesting!

Nothing brings me more joy than knowing once you close the pages to this book, we will be able to stay connected through some of these valuable resources.

Find out what The Hope Shot has to offer by scanning their QR code.

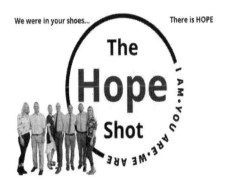

Find out what Brad at Sober Motivation has to offer by scanning his QR code.

Visit my friends below and find out why they are a constant go-to for my recovery!

Resources for Hope and Healing

Help is within reach; you are *not* alone! There are several 12-step communities that offer support not only for the addict, but for the loved ones as well!

The impact that addiction has on the family unit is complex and varied. In most cases, you will find that the entire ecosystem of the addict has been disrupted. Loved ones of the addict are forced to adopt unhealthy coping mechanisms as they try to find balance. This often leads to blurred boundaries and co-dependency.

Some of the resources listed below are also for families in recovery and can provide a greater chance at success for everyone involved.

Alcoholics Anonymous
www.aa.org
www.alcoholicsanonymous.com
1-800-839-1686

Find an AA Meeting
www.aa-meetings.com
www.addict-help.com/aa-zoom-meeting

Al-Anon/Alateen
www.al-anon.org
1-888-4AL-ANON (1-888-425-2666)

Narcotics Anonymous
www.na.org
1-818-773-9999

National Suicide Prevention Hotline
www.suicidepreventionlifeline.org
1-800-273-8255
24-hour access: text/call 988

Find a Treatment Center Near You:
Substance Abuse and Mental Health Services Administration (SAMHSA)
www.findtreatment.gov *or* www.samhsa.gov
1-800-662-HELP (1-800-622-4357)

Sobber Buddy App
www.yoursoberbuddy.com

The Twelve Steps of Alcoholics Anonymous

1. We admitted we were powerless over alcohol—that our lives had become unmanageable.
2. Came to believe that a Power greater than ourselves could restore us to sanity.
3. Made a decision to turn our will and our lives over to the care of God as we understood Him.
4. Made a searching and fearless moral inventory of ourselves.
5. Admitted to God, to ourselves, and to another human being the exact nature of our wrongs.
6. Were entirely ready to have God remove all these defects of character.
7. Humbly asked Him to remove our shortcomings.
8. Made a list of all persons we had harmed, and became willing to make amends to them all.
9. Made direct amends to such people wherever possible, except when to do so would injure them or others.
10. Continued to take personal inventory and when we were wrong promptly admitted it.
11. Sought through prayer and meditation to improve our conscious contact with God as we understood Him, praying only for knowledge of His will for us and the power to carry that out.
12. Having had a spiritual awakening as the result of these steps, we tried to carry this message to alcoholics, and to practice these principles in all our affairs.

The Twelve Promises of Alcoholics Anonymous

1. If we are painstaking about this phase of our development, we will be amazed before we are halfway through.
2. We are going to know a new freedom and a new happiness.
3. We will not regret the past nor wish to shut the door on it.
4. We will comprehend the word serenity, and we will know peace.
5. No matter how far down the scale we have gone, we will see how our experience can benefit others.
6. That feeling of uselessness and self-pity will disappear.
7. We will lose interest in selfish things and gain interest in others.
8. Self-seeking will slip away.
9. Our whole attitude and outlook upon life will change.
10. Fear of people and of economic insecurity will leave us.
11. We will intuitively know how to handle situations which used to baffle us.
12. We will suddenly realize that God is doing for us what we could not do for ourselves.

Unity is a beautiful thing! Let's stay connected!

Facebook: Sober-Now

Instagram: sober.so.now.what (Sober-Now)

Website: www.sober-now.com

Interested in me speaking to your group?
Email me: Melissa@sober-now.com

Scan QR Code for my social media pages and to pay it forward:
linktr.ee/sobernow

Are you ready for the next book in the

I'm Sober... So Now What series?

COMING SOON – WINTER 2024

Stay sober and stay tuned...

Made in the USA
Middletown, DE
03 August 2023

36010084R00075